WRETIRE WRONG:

A Coloring Book to misinform your Golden Years

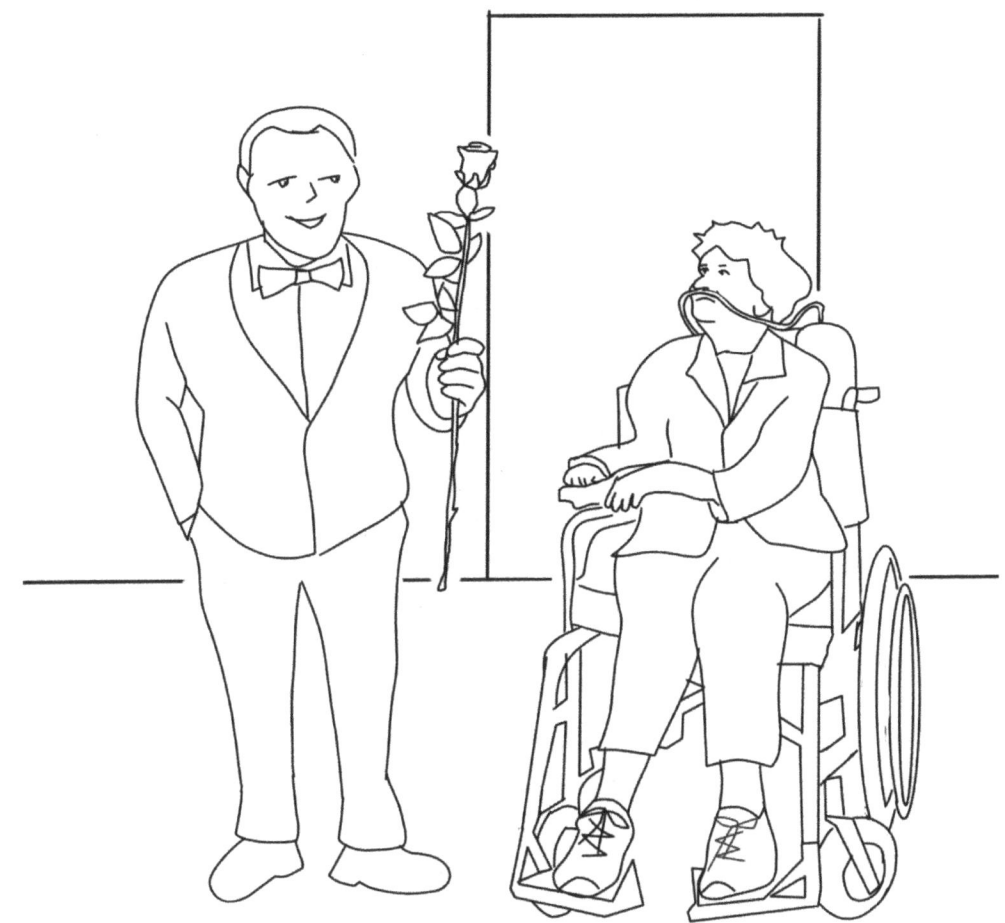

Christopher Gallagher, MD
Illustrations by: Bryce Westervelt

Copyright C Gallagher Consulting Inc.
© 2016

Copyright C Gallagher Consulting Inc.
© 2016

All rights reserved

ISBN 978-0-9976756-0-3

Introduction:

Ah retirement.
    Reaping the fruits of your labors.
    You've worked like an industrious ant all these years, now you can laugh at the careless grasshoppers.
    Sleeping in, sipping Chablis, soaking up the sunsets.
    Cruise the world, conquer mountains, cuddle the grandkids.
    Sound good? Damned Skippy it sounds good.

    If you do it right.

    And there is no lack of "Guides to Retiring Right".
    Retirement finances? Bookstores (the few remaining ones), have shelf after shelf of how to manage your money. Online? 10,000 books, 100,000 websites, a million blogs – all showing you how to steer your greenbacks as you go gray.

    Retirement location? As the stars in the nighttime desert sky, so also are the options for where to live in retirement. Abroad? Try Malta, or Costa Rica, or Uruguay, or you name it. Tax friendly states? Sure, they're all over the map. Stay put? An option. The gypsy life, dump everything and Airbnb your way around the planet? Why not? RV around the US of A? Rent? Snowbird? The possibilities are endless.

    Retirement lifestyle? Troll around on the Internet or just ask around, and you can get 1,001 options. From low-stress, low-maintenance (go fishing in the neighborhood park) to the nth degree of madcap (marathon on all seven continents, and yes, that means Antarctica too).
Finances, housing, lifestyle – it's all there for the soon-to-be-retired.

    If you do it right.

    But where's the fun in that?
    Who are the most interesting characters in books? The ones who do things wrong, of course. Did people buy Fifty Shades of Gray because the billionaire guy played by the usual romantic rules? If Scarlett O'Hara had behaved like a shy, retiring southern belle, would
anyone have read Gone with the Wind? If Scout had minded her own business, people wouldn't have been gobbling up To Kill a Mockingbird for the last half century.

    Who jumps to mind in movies? Luke Skywalker in Star Wars? Well, yeah, fine, follow the Force, sure, we get it. Darth Vader? Booyah! There's a character we'll never forget. The FBI agent in Silence of the Lambs? Sure, she was good (what was her name though?). But Hannibal Lecter? Yeah, he's a cannibal to remember. Dorothy and her entourage were all sugar and spice and everything nice in The Wizard of Oz, but that Wicked Witch of the West stole the show, no doubt.

    So if you do it right, well, meh.
    But if you do it wrong, well, that's where you'll find all the zing.
    So let's do it wrong and color in all that zing.
    Let's Wretire Wrong.

Bob places deed on 23 red.

No better way to assure a comfortable dotage. Take the sweat of your brow, from a lifetime of work, no less, and make a beeline to the casino!

All those mornings you got up before dawn, all those nights you crawled back after dark.

Now put every last penny on the line for one big spin of that roulette wheel, come on, live a little! Go big or go home, right?

Ladies and gentlemen – Place your bets!

Joe puts retirement to good use by regular exercise

Come on, you've broken your back all these years, time to take a load off, put your keester on a comfy sofa, pop those feet up, and reach for the soda and chips.

And some more.

And some more.

If you need to get your heart rate up to a healthy rate, why, you've got the channel changer right there! Tune in those "adult channels" and you'll have all the cardiac workout you need.

Too much work to go to the fridge and get a refill? Don't sweat it, pretty soon they'll have in-home drones that can do that for you too!

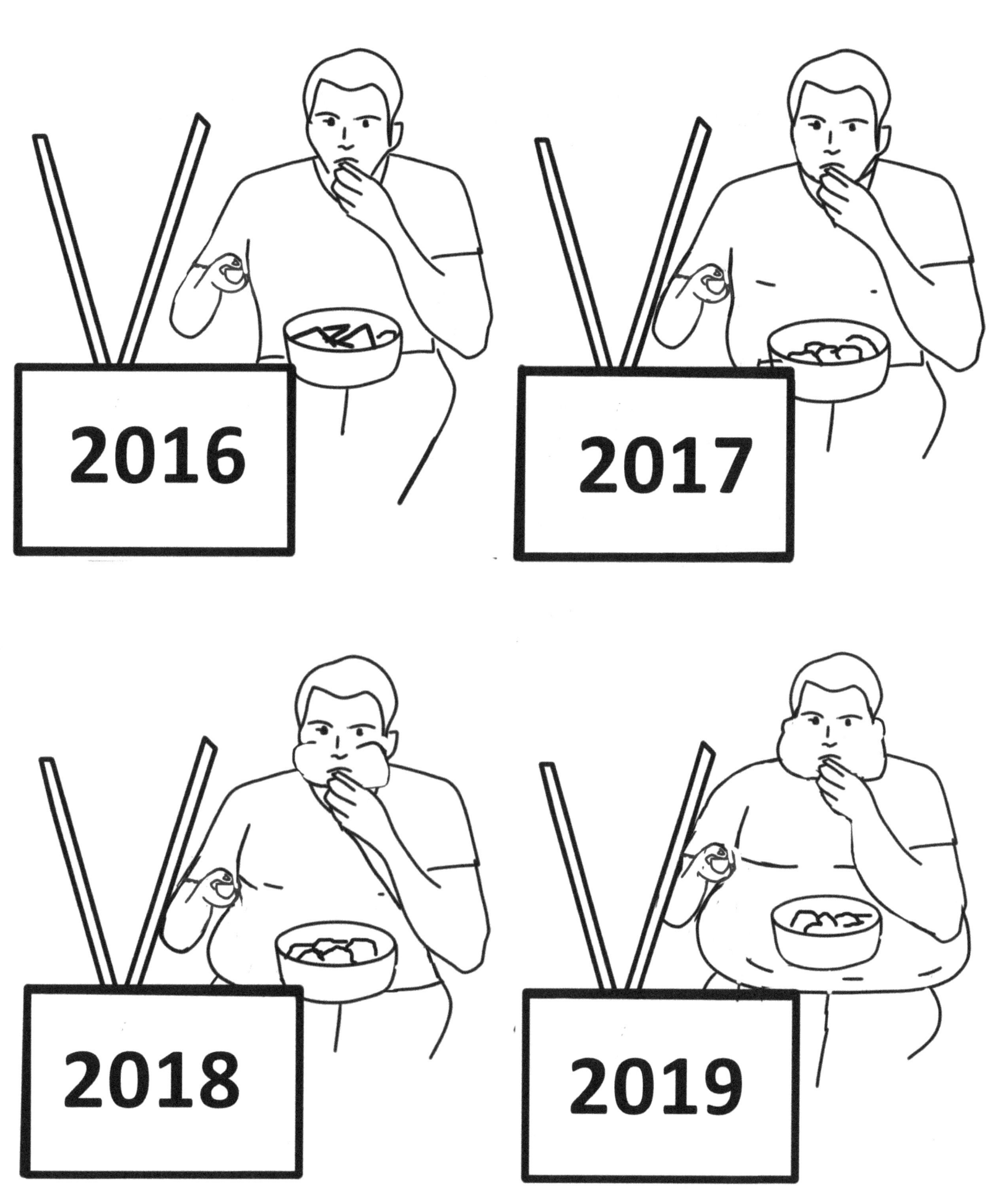

Terry Keeps Working Like a Maniac 'til the End

Terry figures there's never enough money saved, so plans on going full time 'til she's 106. "THEN I'll have enough money!"

Psst, don't look now Terry, but you won't make it to 106. Sorry to be the one to break it to you.

But you go ahead and keep going and going and going, pushing that big ol' rock up that hill.

You'll be an inspiration to all of us.

All of us watching from our recliners.

Mary trusts no one so buries money in back yard.

That's right, Mary, you keep that money good and close
where you can keep an eye on it.

Banks? Pffftt!

Investment plans? Fooey!

They're all in cahoots with the revenuers anyways.
No, you seal up those Kerr® jars real good,
you dig *good* and deep and keep your dough
safe, safe, safe in that backyard there.

No one will *ever* think to look there.
Now stay alert and keep that shotgun handy.

Susie Sweats Market as She Hypermanages and Worries

What? What's that? Dow futures down by 0.01% for tomorrow? Wait, that will require some rebalancing.

Susie is on the case, tuned in, online, cloud-based and ready for action with her multi-synced retirement management juggernaut office space.

Sleep? What, and miss out on what happened in Asia yesterday (or tomorrow, how does that international dateline work again?).

Go outside and get fresh air? Never, oil might tick up just as she leaves, and she'd miss out on her deepwater drilling play.

Wait, what's this? Interest rates look like they're making a move, gotta go!

Bill Says Why Save Anything, Snag a Sugar Momma.

Love is, has always been, and will always be a many-splendored thing. Never more so than when it serves the retirement plans of our lucre-seeking Lothario.

Why put money in a savings account or 401K? Spend that money on flowers for the moneyed honeys at the local nursing home!

Romance, a whirlwind courtship and wedding (before the estate-contesters get wind of Bill's shenanigans), then it's just a question of switching around this heart pill for that sugar pill and voila!

Retirement planning with the aid of Cupid's arrow. How sweet it is.

Winnifred places Faith in Factory

"My Dad worked at this factory for 40 years, and they took care of him when his golden years rolled around. They will certainly take care of me when it's my time."

You go girl, of course they will!

America's industrialists will always put the welfare of their workers first!

So keep the faith Winnifred, and rest assured that your retirement will be taken care of by the warm and loving embrace of your employers.

They dare to care.

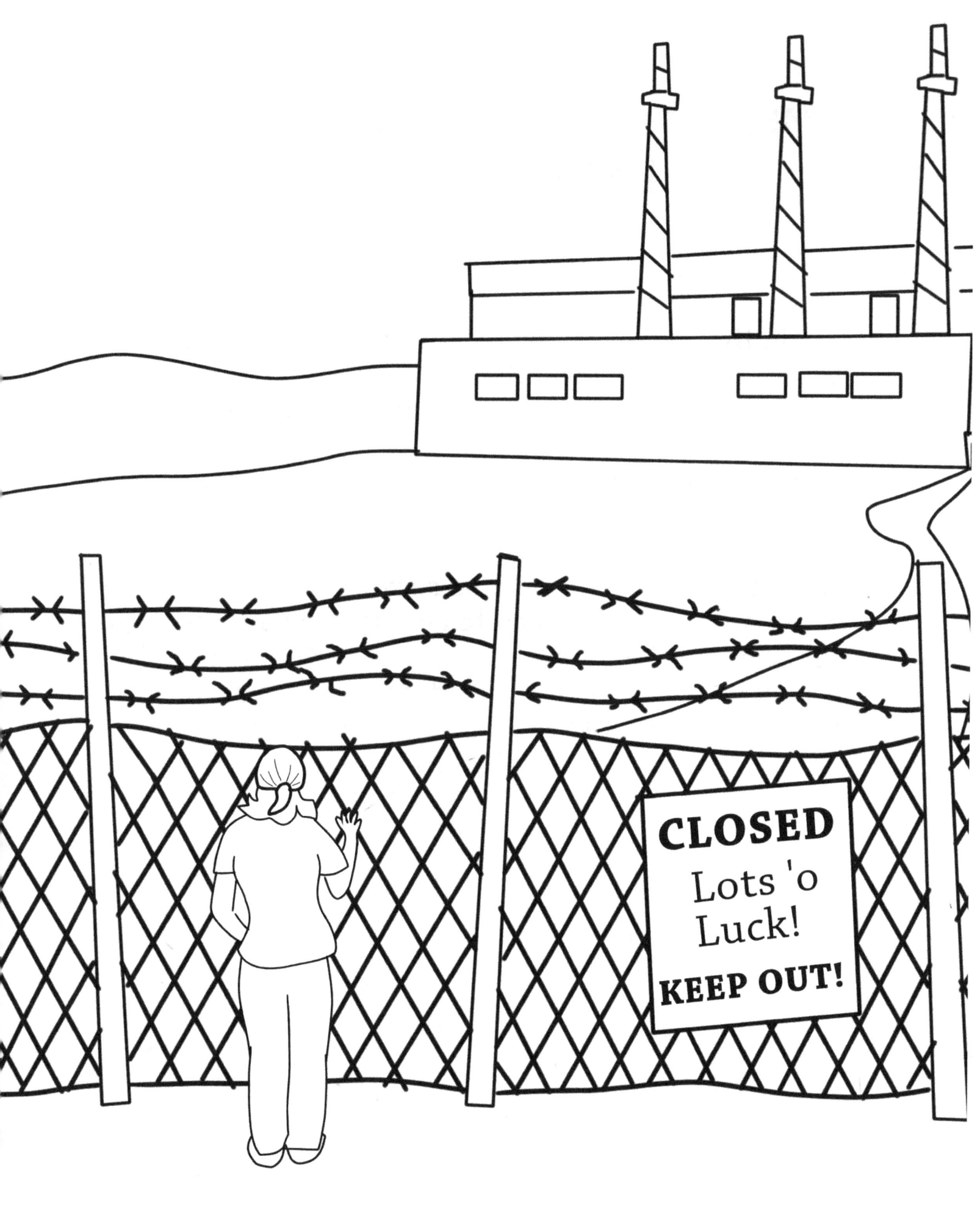

Jeff is going to inherit 150 million from Nigerian Heir.

Man, some guys have *all* the luck!

While the rest of us "strut and fret our hour upon the stage" (certainly upon the *financial* stage), Jeff lucks out with this out-of-the-blue e-mail.

Who knew he had a tenuous (but lucrative!) link to some loaded muckety muck way over in Nigeria?

Jeff laughs at the rest of us suckers, tucking away our nickels and dimes, hoping to one day score ourselves a retirement FEMA surplus hut outside Kissimmee. Jeff is heading straight for easy street as soon as he sends the Nigerian bank the 10,000 dollar administrative fee.
Lucky Jeff!

Kurt Figures One Step Outside Law is OK

A lifetime of toeing the line, helping little old ladies across the street, and becoming the youngest Eagle Scout in county history does not *necessarily* set you up for comfort in your later years.
At least it didn't for Kurt.

So, OK, one *little* step outside the lines, just one, couldn't hurt, could it? Just a tiny detour from righteousness to the dark side to cook up
a little, bitty nest egg.

You know what Kurt, no one reading this book will judge you harshly for such a move.

Hey, you do what you have to do to retire, go for it.
Hope it works out well for you, Kurt.

Gwendolyn Lives it Up

Spend your money wisely. Budget appropriately.
Keep tabs on what you've got and how
you can stre-e-e-etch it out during
(what could be a long) retirement.

Right?

Guess again, says Gwendolyn!

Gwen took one look at what she'd saved and said,
"Let's PA-A-A-ARTY!"

Hunky dudes peeling grapes and fanning her with
ostrich feathers as she rolls down the river in her own
little Cleopatra re-enactment? Boo-yah!
This is retirement the way it's *supposed* to be done.

Hop on board, Gwen's got the bar tab covered and she's
got a foot masseuse 24/7.

YORO – You only retire once!

Steve takes up extreme sports

Who ever remembers the cautious ones, the risk-averse, the safe?

No one.

Steve wants to carve a place in history with his retirement. Extreme life, here we come!

Zipline the Grand Canyon, check.

Hang glide over an erupting volcano, check.

Hey, anyone can solo on Everest. It's been done by blind people, people with disabilities, kids, oldsters.

But on roller skates?

Go for it Steve! Take that extreme lifestyle of yours to the edge, and beyond!

Carla Switches to e-cigs in Front of gas Station

Maybe those e-cigarettes really are the way to go.
Carla has been slow-dancing with death all these years
by smoking regular cigarettes.

But now she's about to embrace retirement and she
sure doesn't want it cut short by those nasty
tobacco-stuffed coffin nails.
(It is so hard to quit, those high-and-mighty
non-smokers will never understand.)

Well, The National Enquirer (on sale at this very gas
station) says the e-cigs are safe, and that's good
enough for Carla.

Never one to "put off 'til tomorrow what she can
do today," Carla starts the ignition device
on her much-safer-for-you e-cigarette.

While she's filling up her tank.

Quint takes up Animal Husbandry

Retirement is all about going out and living life, not sitting around and watching life pass you by.

Enter Quint.

During his working days, he'd park in front of that 60-inch HDTV and watch Animal Planet every night.

But no more. Retirement gives him the opportunity to go from observing those exotic animals to bending them to his will!

That's it Quint! Show them who is the alpha animal in this pride.

Who know, maybe Quint will have his own show soon on Animal Planet!

Tim uses whispered tips to guide investment strategy

"Hey, Tim! My cousin met a guy at a conference who said he knows that Greenland is about to uncover..."

"Psst, Tim, don't tell anyone this, but *the government* has to sell all their platinum because..."

"Oh Tim, I'm glad I ran into you, this hasn't made the news yet, but..."

Tim was blessed with two extremely receptive ears, always ready to receive the latest hot tip (invariably delivered in an excited whisper) that NO ONE else knows about.

What better way to guide your investment decisions? Whispered tips, back alleys, secret plots.
That's the ticket.

Let the other schmucks be satisfied with their piddly returns.

Tim's gonna make a killing because, get a little closer so I can whisper it to you too, he just heard that...

Judy assumes she'll die young so assumes doesn't need to save

There's never time to do things right (like save),
but there's always time to do things later (like save).

"Why save today?" Judy thought,
"I can always save tomorrow!"

"Besides, the way I eat (if it's not deep fat fried, it has no taste), drink (Mad Dog 20/20 complements any occasion), and cat around (marital vows are best thought of as suggestions), I never have to worry about growing old! I'll be shot dead by a jealous wife long before I have to reach into any retirement piggy bank!"

Alas, poor Judy, I knew her well.

Between an iron constitution, an epically resilient liver, and a clutch of wives with poor marksmanship, Judy has outlived her expectations, her romantic rivals, and, of course, her money.

Harold has plenty of time to shop and gets his stuff by drone.

People do all sorts of things at night – from meeting lovers to discovering asteroids to tunneling out of prison.

Harold grabs his credit card with one hand, his phone with other, and goes Late Night Infomercial Shopping.

Gut Buster, Ab-Wizard, Brutish Bicep Builder – "here's my credit card number, expiration date, and that little 3 number thingie."

Videos showing Dance Exercises, Bebop Weight Loss, and Yoga-Set-to-Mozart? Sign Harold up.

Shiny cookware, non-stick burger grills, insta-Caramel Corn Popper? Yes, yes, a thousand times yes!
Since Harold's retired and doesn't need to wake up early, he can shop all night long!

The best thing? The next day, Harold gets to watch the airborne flotilla of drones bringing all his late night loot right to his front door!

Caitlin Says Who Needs Insurance

"Insurance? Might as well pile up your money and have a bonfire with it," Caitlin says. "I'm on optimist!"

Indeed Caitlin is an optimist. And why not? Nice house, nice neighborhood, and Caitlin *herself* is nice, so what could go wrong?

"If there is any cosmic justice, then bad Karma goes to those who bring it on themselves, and blowing your retirement money on some stupid insurance policy just *begs* for bad Karma."

Otto uses cash from his new credit cards to get lots of Lotto tickets.

Otto was always a little too strapped for cash to play the Lotto the way it was meant to be played (Otto has a system, which he prefers to keep to himself, thank you very much).

Thank goodness he found out that he can take cash advances on his credit card!

And how about snapping up a few more credit cards and snagging some cash advances on them too!

Yes!

Now, on the 3rd, 7th, and 22nd of every month (OK, so he may let you peak at his method), he goes with 2 if it's raining, adds a 7 if he hits a red light at the nearest intersection, then flips a coin to decide the other...

And those credit card cash advances help him to double down the next week if he doesn't win!
It's a sure thing!

Julia thinks the slicker the investment expert, the better.

Whoa, this guy must be good. Just look at that bling. Diamonds in his watch. Italian-cut suit. Alligator shoes. Grill.

The full Monte.

This financial advisor must be the bee's knees, how else could he have landed all this dandy stuff?

Rest easy, Julia, you can know that this trustworthy fellow always puts your interests first.

Don't fret for a minute where he got all that money from. Or who he got it from.

Bret jumps all over the late night get rich quick schemes

Forget shopping on late night television, how about striking the Mother Lode on late night television!
Bret is chomping at the bit to sign up for those sure-fire moneymakers. What better way to turn "retirement" into "deluxe retirement".

Look at this guy, he started out with only a bottle cap for collateral and now he owns 10 properties!
And one of those is Buckingham Palace!

Bret says "Sign me up!"

But wait, there's another one, look at that guy on the yacht, surrounded by a bevy of beauties, holding a glass of Dom Perignon in his hand
(well, he says it's Dom Perignon).

And he made all this money flipping houses.

"Easy as flipping coins", the man says, "and he's got the yacht to prove it!"

All aboard the USS Easy Street for Bret.

Paula Joins a Cult that Promises Riches

All of Paula's working life, she had to toe the party line
and do what her bosses told her to do
(she is not alone in that regard!).

Now she's retired and, well, old habits die hard.

The group she joined seemed so nice.
And best of all, this group promised hefty dividends if
you just "do what you are told".

Well, why not, says Paula. Why the heck not.

Joy uses her new language skills in retirement in Tijuana.

What better way to see the world than to get immersed in it.
Learn the language, get off the beaten path, get right out there and mix it up with the natives. That's retirement living at its absolute acme and pitch.
And that's just what Joy is all about.
Learned a little Spanish online, practiced with a friend, snagged a translation App, bingo!
Now all she had to do was avoid the touristy areas and plunge into the heart of Tijuana, all by her adventurous lonesome, to get some up close and personal time with these fine citizens.
Ole!

Tony doesn't believe all that hooey about taking care of heart

Modern medicine, right, what do they know?
Tony knows a guy whose second cousin's uncle smoked like a chimney, had bacon and eggs (fried in the bacon grease, mind you) every day for breakfast, and lived to be 102.

Sounds like the perfect recipe for an enjoyable retirement to Tony!

So you can have your skinny latte, just get out of the way as Tony reaches for the heavy whipping cream. And you don't have to worry about him taking the last tub of vegan margarine – it's pure Wisconsin butter that Tony's smearing on his toast, thank you very much.

Bon appetit Tony!

Lois, in retirement, thinks I can't get preggers so I can't get STD's.

Lois didn't work in the biologic sciences, so her grasp of what goes on...er..."down there" may not be exactly razor sharp.

But she's not worrying about such trifles, because it's retirement time and that means the funmobile is in gear and ready to roll!

In her swinging adult community, no one is holding back. Hey, you never know when that cosmic "Repo Man" may come along and sweep away all your earthly cares, so you might as well get as many earthly pleasures as you can!

As Lois sees it, since she's had the change of life, that means "no way I can get pregnant", so let's roll.
And if I "can't catch the pregnant bug, then I can't catch any other bugs there either, right?"

Sure Lois, I think you got it all figured out just right.
Enjoy!

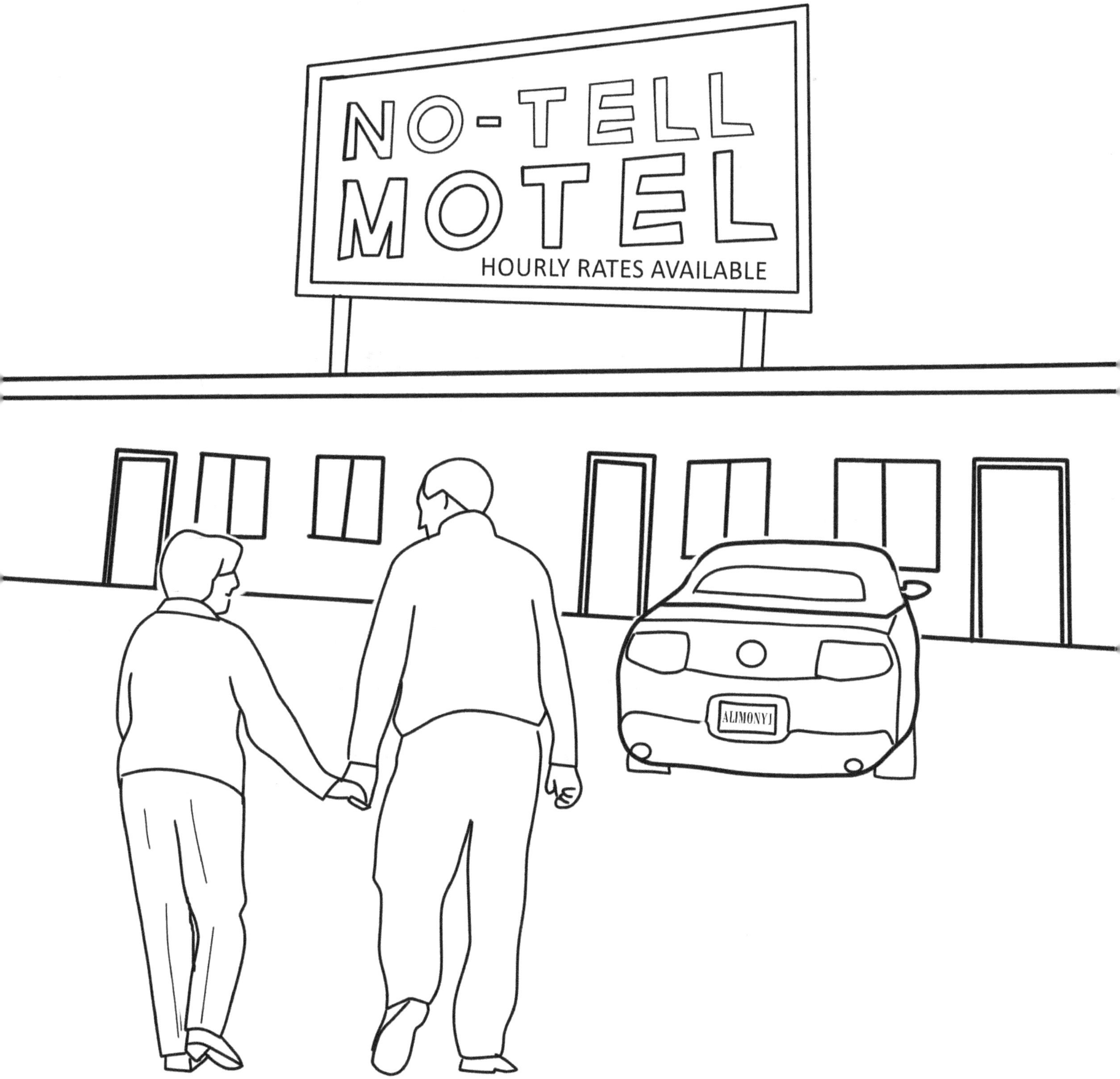
NO-TELL
MOTEL
HOURLY RATES AVAILABLE
ALIMONYJ

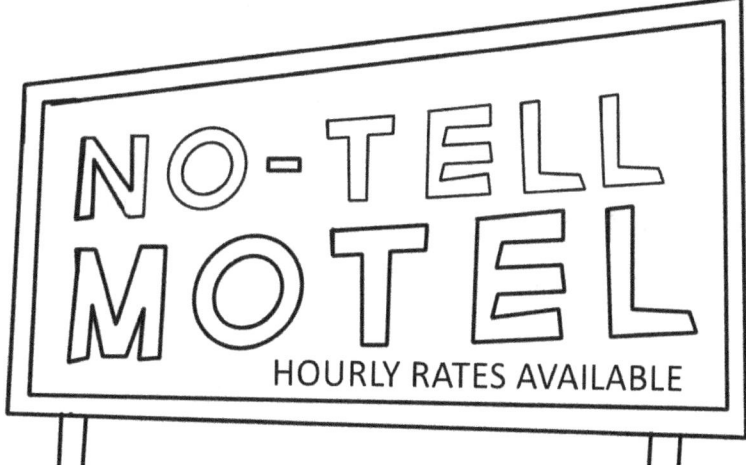

Now that Jack has time, he can do fireworks in his back yard.

Retirement means indulging in your favorite activities.
Jack has always gone to fireworks shows before,
why not run his own show.

How hard can it be?

He's seen the guys shooting those fireworks off,
doesn't look like any of them had picked up Nobel
prizes in Oslo lately.

So what the heck, let' light up the night sky.
Like any good do-it-yourselfer, Jack knows that
"you learn the most by troubleshooting yourself"
(which may be an ironic way
of phrasing things as we will see)

One of those darned supercharged extra-gunpowdered
rockets seems to be having a little trouble coming out of
the tube.

Hmm, go fix it Jack!

Ken Figures the Loan Sharks Will Cut Him Some Slack

Ken has worked the pity angle to great effect
in retirement.

"But I'm on a fixed income," he'll whine,
then lay on the big puppy eyes.

Works like a charm!

This "being a senior" has worked financial wonders, from
those early-bird specials at the family restaurants,
to the discount on movie tickets, to mooching
a few bucks off his kids.

So now Ken's had a little, bitty run of bad luck
with the ponies.

And, OK, maybe he had to arrange some higher-interest
loans that don't exactly appear in the books.

But those guys seemed so so eager to lend him that
money at the track. Surely they will give me a break.
After all, you are a senior, on a fixed income.

Try that on for size, Ken,

I'm sure they'll see things in a fav favorable light.

Chris doesn't have to be sober for work so drinks 24/7

What's that they say for pilots?
8 hours between bottle and throttle?

Hey, Chris is retired, no need to be hemmed in by any "when you can and can't drink" rules anymore.

No dangerous machinery, no problem if the words are slurred, no problem if the breath smells like pure Kentucky bourbon. As long as Chris can stagger from the living room to the bedroom – it's all good.

What better way to spend the golden years than in a boozy haze?

Bottoms up, Chris!

Cary doesn't worry about embarrassing himself on social media.

In the bad old days (ie, when he was working), Cary had to keep a tight rein on his social media clowning.

Not so now that the curtain has fallen on work. Who cares who's watching anymore?

So Cary can cut loose and post all those wild and wacky things he's always been holding in check.

Streaking at his grandson's kindergarten graduation. Chugging flaming tequila shots with the underage drinkers.

Getting too friendly with the goats at the petting zoo.

It's all just fine, Cary, live it up, keep that camera rolling, and post away to your heart's content.

Gracie has all the time in the world, so why not drop in to visit anytime.

"Hey, guess what?" Gracie says to her cousins, who were getting ready to take her to the airport so she could finally leave them after her unannounced 3-week visit, "I don't have to go! I just changed my flight to next month!"

Gracie slipped into retirement and just as quickly slipped into her "visiting shoes".

Now that she has all the time in the world, what better way to spend it than dropping in on everybody and staying.

And staying.

And staying.

That way she can really get to know them after all these years.

Isn't that great?

Maybe Gracie will pop in and visit you soon too!

Roberta doesn't think the shark bite from early withdrawal will hurt.

It's not quite time to retire, and Roberta would sure like to do a little shopping.

And there is that retirement money just sitting there, taking up space.

Hmmm.

Why not maybe, just this once (well, OK, maybe more than once) just take that financial ladle and just dip a little bit into all that retirement swag.

Can't hurt, can it? It's my money, after all, goodness knows I earned it.

There is that little, bitty, teeny 10% penalty for early withdrawal. Well fine, so what, I lose a few dimes (I mean a dime is 10% of a dollar, that's one way of looking at it).

And yes there's the taxes.

But it's just like Monopoly® money anyways, so just take it Roberta.

So you might get a few little shark bites out of your money, so what?

Neil's a real homebody so why not do online gambling.

The computer revolution unfolded during Neil's working life.

Along comes e-mail – POOF, regular mail and written memos disappear.

Along comes the Internet – POOF, there goes trips to the stacks in libraries to do research.

Shopping, traveling, everything!
And what's this latest Internet craze to catch the recently-retired Neil's eyes?

Online gambling! POOF – there go trips to Vegas and Atlantic City. Who needs to fight your way through airport security, wedge into economy seats, and check into dubious hotel rooms?

You can gamble from the comfort of your own home!
Lost? Double down, my man, win it back! And you can do this in your pyjamas!
Ooo, lost again.

Keep going Neil, you're sure to win if you double down again this time.
Right?

Ernest decides retirement is good time to bring long dormant muscles back to life.

"Start low, go slow", the doctors say.

"Work with a professional before you start an exercise regime," the personal trainers say.

"Use common sense," Ernest's wife says.

"To hell with all of you!" Ernest shouts. "There might be a little water under the bridge since I've gone to the gym, but I was quite the specimen back in the day!"

So Ernest throws off the shackles of well-meaning advice and bulldozes straight into the gym, picking up where he left off 45 years and 95 pounds ago.

His will be a physically fit retirement, and the time to start is today!

And a ONE, a TWO...

Tina makes a big hit telling everyone she's cashing out

Tina has a heart as big as Montana.

Tina has never heard a sob story that didn't shake her right down to the core of her existence.

Tina just cashed out her retirement dough and let every Sad Sack and Patty Pitiful know exactly how much she has.

What's this? Newfound popularity?

Tina had no idea she had so many friends. Come one, come all!

What's this you say? No, you need how much? It's the least I can do.

And what's this you say? Well, every little bit helps. And you, and you, and you too?

Darryl brags about his brilliant investing

Boy there's nothing people enjoy more than hearing about all your good fortune.

Darryl is leaping into a featherbed of a retirement, full of great big fluffy piles of dollars from all the brilliant moves he has made.

His friends never tire of hearing about how well Darryl did, or, at least, that's how Darryl reads it.

"Hey, I was in on the Google IPO, do you know how many times it's split?"

"Then my uncle leaves me this rundown apartment building in Brooklyn Heights, now the place has gentrified and I've made bank!"

"No kidding I shorted all the oil stocks before they tanked, who knew there was that much money to be made!"

Darryl's friends seem eager to help him enjoy a long and happy retirement.

Color Isabella's last two nickels shiny silver. Make them sparkle because they're all she has left after providing Junior with a Cadillac education.

Isabella thinks nothing is too good for Junior's college education.

Ivy League, private suite in the dorm, car to get to classes, tutors, summer vacations abroad/on cruise ships - the whole nine yards.

Anything to fill her child's mind.

Damn the expenses, full speed ahead!

What a good Mommy!

François colors in our coloring book.

And what could possibly top all these
other retirement scenarios?

Let's go abroad for that answer.

François takes his last few euros and has one final fling.

What better way to cap off retirement?

He colors in Wretire Wrong:
A Coloring Book to Misinform Your Golden Years.

Voila!

Final Word:

We hope François and Darryl and Joy and everybody else in this book has a long and happy retirement - guided by the sage advice we provided here.

We here at Wretire Wrong hope that this book helps you have a long and happy retirement too!

Thanks!

Color in your own sunset years in the space provided below!

If you liked **Wretire Wrong,** try these other books by Christopher Gallagher:

Linguanaut: The Adventure of Learning Foreign Languages.

Sailing through languages is an adventure. Jump on board and see how it's done, then see what amazing things await you. Learn how you can use free material from your old friend the library, from your new friend the Internet, and then go out and make new friends with your new language skills. The author has picked up about a dozen languages, and with them he has helped bring the Berlin Wall down, shown Tiger Moms how to get their kids into the Ivy League, broken bread with the Mozambique Olympic team, and has helped restore smiles to disfigured children in the Andes. All this with languages? Yes! And best of all, you can too. So read on, become a Linguanaut, and sail the adventure-filled realm of foreign languages.

Florida Plates: Who Rented this Car Before Me?

Nearly every rental car has a colorful past. These humorous short stories recount the history of one such rental car – a Camry with Florida plates. The itinerant occupants are as diverse as one can imagine... And their human peccadilloes range from the poignant to the bizarre to the ludicrous. Who knows where your rental car has been, and with whom? An entertaining read for your on-the-road, vacation, or just plain at-home amusement.

The Cellars of Marcelcave: A Yank Doctor in the BEF.

Before America went to war in 1917 to make the world "safe for democracy, "Uncle Sam sent more than 1,500 doctors to fill the depleted ranks of the British Army. Among these volunteers was Ben Gallagher, twenty-eight, fresh from his internship. With a clinician's eye and a historian's sense he saw the "war to end all wars" from a front line aid post. He survived several hairbreadth escapes as well as a successful escape from a prisoner of war camp. But only Ben's shoes make it to freedom! Ben's encounters with wounded British, the famous Baron von Richtofen, and a German intelligence officer bring the conflict to life.

Interested in having Mr. Westervelt do illustrations for you? Contact him through fiverr.com. Look for bryceartist. Let me give him the shout out he deserves! Pleasant, timely, and best of all, he gets on your wavelength and understands just what you need in your illustrations. I loved working with him, you will too!

Interested in having Dr. Gallagher give a talk at your retirement group (you can see he gives good advice!), company's annual meeting (he's sure to get a laugh, even if he doesn't know much about your company!), or language interest group (you don't meet many people who are fluent in a half-dozen languages, or is it a dozen?), drop him a line:

    e-mail: ChrisGallagher1988@gmail.com

    snail mail (does anyone even use that anymore?) in case you're retro:
    Christopher Gallagher, MD
    19 Beacon Hill Dr
    Stony Brook, NY 11790

    I'd love to hear from you!
    Happy Trails and a Happier Retirement!

WRETIRE WRONG:

A Coloring Book to misinform your Golden Years

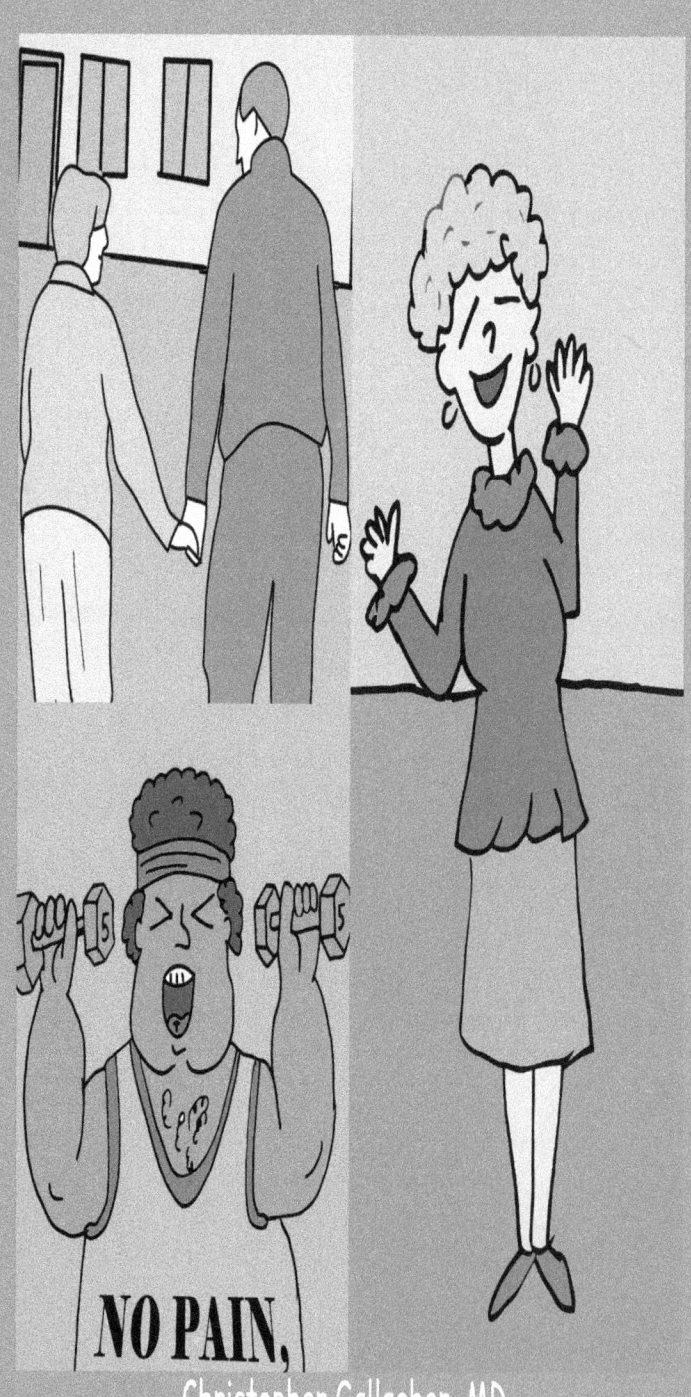

Wretire Wrong

There's no shortage of good retirement advice. Wise people telling sage listeners how to do the right thing in their September years.

Where's the fun in that?

Hop on board Wretire Wrong and take the misguided ride of your life! Then pick up some colored pencils and immortalize these misguided precepts with your own artistic touch.

What can you learn from Wretire Wrong?

Bury your cash in your backyard!
Whispered stock tips in hallways are the best research!
By all means get more Lotto tickets!
8 AM? Bottoms up! Who needs sobriety?

So sharpen your pencils, roll up your sleeves, and get ready to squander a lifetime of hard work. It's time to Wretire Wrong!

Christopher Gallagher, MD
Illustrations by: Bryce Westervelt